Why Farm Wives
AGE FAST
No. II

Editor
Eleanor Jacobs

Layout and Design
Lori Abramowski

Cover Design and Cartoons
Dave Carpenter

Production
**Sally Manich, Ellen Baltes,
Tom La Fleur, Henry de Fiebre**

———————

International Standard Book Number 0-89821-074-7

Library of Congress Catalog Card Number 86-61012

© 1986, Reiman Publications, Inc.,
5400 South 60th St., Greendale, Wisconsin 53129

TABLE OF CONTENTS

Who Ever Said Mud Packs Make You Beautiful?

By Frances Reidlinger of Barnard, Missouri

My husband, Charles, is a type you might recognize. When he decides to sort hogs, he means *now*—not after school when the boys can help...but now, when only Mom is available! His impatience sometimes leads to murky work for me...and plenty of laughs for him.

"Hon, the hog market looks good today. Let's sort out a few and run them to market," he mentioned subtly not long ago.

What could I say to a man who is all smiles and says, "hon"?

"Of course," I replied with a dubious smile.

Now any farm wife knows how contrary hogs can be when you want to sort them for market. And to complicate the situation, I was very pregnant and very clumsy at the time. In fact, I could have fallen over my own shadow at that point.

None of that stopped me from pulling on my boots and heading toward the barn lot side by side with my smiling husband, who reassured me, "This ought to be a snap, hon. We'll only cut out one load."

Ah, only *one* load—25 pigs. Not bad, I thought to myself, all the while knowing it's never as simple as it sounds.

As we entered the lot through the small side gate, mud oozed around my boots, and hogs gathered around my ankles. (Ours were the nosy, tame kind that never moved out of the way of anything.) Charles slipped over and checked to see how many hogs were out in the west lot while I stood for inspection. Then he motioned me to ease my way around the hogs, and we would shoo them into the barn before we ran the others in.

This went well, and our confidence grew.

With the hogs safely in the barn lot, we let the first bunch out of the barn and began sorting...all the while battling the mud that ebbed and flowed beneath us.

I slipped and slid as we sorted hogs into a temporary pen built out into the lot. Once a few were in there, we shooed them on into the barn and shut the door.

We had just two or three left to make 25. Almost home safe! But as I wobbled around the murky lot, I wished those were in the barn, too!

Finally Charles shooed the last two in my direction, and I

5

moved to head them toward the opening of our pen.

One big fellow, though, had a different idea. He obviously had no intention of going to market that day, and with the speed only a determined hog can muster, he took aim and tried to run right through me. As I sidestepped, my feet slid! I sprawled face down in the sloppiest mud puddle in the barnyard.

My *poor* husband nearly choked trying not to laugh as he asked, "Are you all right, hon?"

"Yes, I'm okay," I replied as I lumbered to my feet, dripping mud.

"You're sure—I mean, the baby?"

"I'm okay, dear," I sputtered through mud-slick lips.

Finally he couldn't contain himself any longer and burst into a laugh that shook him nearly to tears.

As he shook, I grew indignant. After all, I knew I wasn't a raving beauty, especially in a mud pack, but the situation wasn't as funny as he seemed to think.

Finally his laughter quieted, and he managed to tell me to go to the house and clean up. He would load the hogs into the truck, and by then I should be ready to go with him to market.

As I trudged from the lot, I took one last glance at Charles, catching sight of his shoulders still quivering with laughter. I stomped toward the house, where I peeled off my outer, mud-dripping clothes on the porch and dashed for the bathroom.

Well, one look in the mirror, and I could see why my husband had laughed so heartily.

There I stood, almost unrecognizable. Slits of eyes peered through gray-black mud that coated my whole body.

As the last of the mud drained down the tub, I resolved that when hog-sorting time next arrived, Charles could just wait for the boys to get home from school...at least if "my condition" was unchanged.

Luckily for Charles, on the way to the market he voiced the same opinion—even though it was accompanied by quivering shoulders!

Black Hole Dilemma

BY JOYCE D. KISLING OF DILLER, NEBRASKA

I see the latest bit of speculation in scientific circles concerns the Black Hole theory. Some learned men believe that way out there in the galaxy are huge empty spots into which everything simply disappears.

Well, I would like to invite a stray scientist or two to our farm. I think we've got a Black Hole right here in Jefferson County.

I had a one-legged pliers and a hammer with a broken claw which I always kept in the tool drawer in the basement. They are gone. No one knows where.

My scissors are missing, too. One of my sons told me he hadn't seen them since he borrowed them to cut his bicycle chain. That was 9 years ago. I don't give up easily, but there are limits to one's patience. Let's face it—those scissors are gone forever.

I did manage to hang on to a vise grip and a screwdriver for a while by welding both items to a 12-ft. log chain which I attached

---

"Food, especially the last piece of pie, vanishes. Peanut butter doesn't stand a chance. But nothing ever happens to broccoli!"

---

to the kitchen cabinet with a combination padlock. I was secure in the knowledge I could dismantle, or repair, anything within a reasonable distance. That dream's dashed now. The only thing left is the cabinet.

Paper disappears on a regular basis. (This may or may not be due to the rather unique filing system I have developed, but we really have no proof one way or the other.) Recently we were audited by our friendly Internal Revenue Service. The agent, bless his fickled heart, firmly believed that at least one person per household should know where all the bodies are buried and asked me to produce our repair bills.

I was certain I had filed them under "D" for Depressing. They weren't there. I looked under "G" for Ghastly. No luck. The IRS man just rubbed his hands gleefully.

Another time I had to find a canceled check to show we had paid a bill. A truly humane company politely offered to ruin our credit rating unless we had it to wave under the computer's mechanical nose. I searched in all the places where I ordinarily keep important documents—behind the refrigerator, under the bed and between the torn jeans which seem to grow like bread dough in the sewing room. We finally had to go to the bank for a duplicate copy.

Food, especially the last piece of pie, vanishes. Cinnamon rolls are hard-hit, too. Peanut butter doesn't stand a chance. Nothing ever happens to broccoli, though.

Before we had teenagers with cars, paper towels were safe. So were window cleaner and vacuum cleaners. I have occasionally recovered my vacuum from the garage, sometimes minus a vital working part, but at least I got it back. What an "Unknown Force" doesn't suck up, it will wreck. Experience teaches this.

Recipes don't last. Cut an interesting one out of a newspaper, and 2 or 3 years later when you want to try it, bingo. Nothing. Gone.

Back when our children were small, shoes were a big problem. We had twins, and when it was time to go to church, we never could come up with enough shoes to go around...four little feet, three little shoes. When we had three children, there were only five shoes. And so on. It was a mystery we couldn't solve, although, as often as not, the toy box ate them. Sometimes it was the lilac bush. We won a battle here and there, but definitely lost the war.

One of our children lost his blanket, which, up until the time of the disappearance, he insisted on dragging behind him wherever he went. The blanket was the ultimate insult to the detergent industry and defied every known method of bringing it back to its original state of grace. It was, in short, an embarrassment. We had visions of the kid graduating high school with that ratty blanket under his arm. Then, one marvelous day, the blanket was gone. The kid is 24 now and still wonders. My lips are sealed.

Flashlights and pocketknives perish. My favorite blouse went about the same time my daughter left for college, but I'm not accusing anyone. The telephone book, nail clippers, half-read magazines and shampoo are casualties. (My personal opinion is that someone is drinking the shampoo, but I could be wrong.)

Pitchforks, scoop shovels and wrenches, car keys, stamps, thermos jugs and chore coats...though some of us have noticed that the first one out is usually the best-dressed. The bathroom tissue is always down to the cardboard cylinder. I'm constantly putting pens back in the pen place, but there's never anything to write with.

I certainly wish whoever is in charge of this type of investigation would get down to business and come up with a solution as soon as possible. But if they come to our farm to check things over, they'd probably disappear, too...into the Black Hole!

You Can Never Have Too Much Sorghum...Can You?

BY EILEEN MILES OF CLINTON, MICHIGAN

Some people will do just about anything for that special, old-fashioned flavor in their food. I should know.

About 2 years ago I used up the last jar of my home-grown sorghum, and I don't mind telling you, I missed it. Store-bought molasses just doesn't compare to the lighter, sweeter stuff we canned years ago. My baked beans, cookies—even my pancakes—were missing that special something after the sorghum ran out.

So last spring I decided the time had come to put up a fresh batch. We'd do it just like we did when our kids were little...plant and harvest it then take it to the mill to be pressed. Then I'd bring

---

" 'You planted the whole acre to sorghum?' my son asked in disbelief. 'That must be 40 rows!' "

---

the sorghum home and can it, and the family could enjoy that unique and delicious taste for years to come.

Besides, there's nothing like a big project to bring a family together; it was just what we needed.

"Better buy a lot of seed," I mumbled to myself as I flipped through the seed catalog. "If we're going to do it, we might as well have enough to last for a few years." (If I'd only known!)

We told our son, who does the farming now, to leave a spot for us in a nearby field for sorghum. He left a generous acre, and since I had a lot of seed, my husband and I planted nearly the entire space.

Just as we finished, my son stopped by. "You planted the whole thing? Isn't that a lot?" he asked.

I just shrugged my shoulders and admired our freshly planted patch.

"Grandpa never planted that much," he continued. "The most I remember him planting was eight or nine rows. You must have 40 rows here."

"Probably," I agreed, and tried to ignore him as he walked away, shaking his head. He'd see that an acre was worth the effort when the family all gathered around the table for a baked bean supper.

When the plants were about waist high and my husband was about to break the hoe handle over his knee in frustration, our daughter-in-law stopped by to see how things were going. She looked over the patch and casually asked, "Where are you going to have it processed?"

"I'm not sure," I replied, not at all worried."There were several places that would press it last time we did it."

"When was the last time, anyway?" she asked.

"Well, let's see. My dad was still alive, so I guess it was about 25 years ago."

Her eyebrows shot up in surprise. She recovered quickly, but for a moment I was sure my daughter-in-law was wondering if insanity ran in our family.

"Well, there's probably a place that still does it," she said. "If not, I've heard it makes great silage. Have you thought of that?"

I wouldn't dignify her question with an answer and went back to supervising the hoeing.

The sorghum was ready at the same time as some other crops, so my son and his family were tied up during our crucial harvest.

"I still have enough jars of sorghum to line one whole wall of my basement from floor to ceiling...that'll last about 18 years!"

No problem! I rounded up all of the neighborhood kids to help, and we began the process of stripping all the leaves off the stalks.

Unfortunately, the sorghum towered a good 4 ft. above the kids' heads. The work was exhausting, and many of them quit after the first hour. The ones who stuck it out were paid by the rows they completed. Already the project was running into more money than I had planned.

After many phone calls, I located a man who would process the sorghum. "I charge by the gallon," he told me over the phone. "It sounds like you'll have about 80 when you're done."

"Eighty gallons?" I said, and then frantically figured in my head. That's 320 qts.!

"Oh, by the way," he continued, "you don't have to strip the leaves. It doesn't make that much difference."

I didn't want to think about it. Instead, I had to think about where I was going to find some more jars!

The next step in the harvest plan was to snip the heads off the 9-ft. stalks. My son and a neighbor stood on a wagon to do this, and I carefully pulled the wagon with the tractor. My husband followed along and snipped off the heads of those stalks that leaned over too far for the wagon crew to reach. Now this was family togetherness, just as I had planned.

But after 4 or 5 hours of this togetherness, tempers grew a bit short. A hot lunch didn't improve things, either. So much for family teamwork.

My husband had found an old corn binder that would save us hours of labor. He bound the already costly crop and left the bundles scattered on the ground.

Just then my uncle came along for a visit. "What's that doing on the ground?" he asked, pointing to the bundles. "You get dirt on them stalks, you'll have dirt in the syrup. Can't get it out unless you strain it."

My husband, by this time, just shrugged his shoulders and continued to work. "Well, what's a little dirt?" I reasoned with myself. "When my kids were little they would take my sorghum cookies out to the sandbox with them. They probably *expect* them to be a little gritty."

Somehow, between all of us, we finally managed to load the 8-ft. bundles onto the truck without dragging them in the dirt too much. It took two overloaded trips to truck the crop for processing.

We watched the man press the stalks and cook the syrup. Then I took the syrup home in buckets to can in jars, and although I started with quarts, as time went on, my jars became bigger and bigger.

It's nearly spring again now, and I've been looking over my seed catalogs. Seeing the picture of a sorghum plant started me thinking. I've used 3 qts. and given away a dozen. I still have enough jars of syrup to line one whole wall of my basement from floor to ceiling. At this rate, I'll have enough sorghum to last me about 18 years.

No, I think I'll sacrifice family togetherness and not plant any this year.

DID NOAH LIVE LIKE THIS?

BY JOYCE WRIGHT OF WOODBURY, KENTUCKY

All children love pets. But I'll bet farm wives and mothers see a wider variety of animal life than any other segment of the population.

Why? Well, for one thing, we can't use the excuse "You don't have any place to keep it." For another, animals are just more available in the country.

I know. I've had my share. And each of them seemed to have some built-in characteristic designed to drive me mad.

My daughter Lynn learned to walk while holding onto "Taffy", my husband's part-collie, part-shepherd stock dog. When Taffy's services as a prop were no longer needed, she appointed herself Lynn's chief companion, baby-sitter and, unfortunately for the milk inspector, bodyguard.

I suppose the child learned from this that animals are nice to have around. Her first complete sentence was, "I want a cat", and everything was downhill from there.

Instead of a cat we settled for "Charley"—a cute, furry rabbit she spotted at the county fair. He was a tiny, delicate creature who grew—overnight—to the size of a compact car. We allowed Lynn to keep Charley indoors for a while, but when it became obvious that he was competing with us for the oxygen, we exiled him to a dog-house in the backyard. There was no need to cage him, at least not for his own protection. He could and did "lick" everything on the farm that threatened to do him harm.

After Charley came "Myrtle", a turtle Lynn caught from the pond. "Wonderful pet," I exclaimed. "It won't eat the house plants or gallop through the halls at night."

But Myrtle had other ways of making life difficult. She was afflicted with wanderlust and, the best we've been able to figure it, her time limit in captivity was something shy of 10 minutes. We graduated to deeper and deeper pans, and still Myrtle shinnied over the sides. And being about the size of a half-dollar, she was nearly impossible to find.

Finally, before going to town one afternoon, we put Myrtle in an aquarium with only a few inches of water and nothing near the edges on which she could climb. When we returned, sure enough—no Myrtle. After 3 days of being careful where we stepped, we gave up, thinking she must have pried open a window and left the house for good.

Then, on the fourth day, a sizable dust ball walked out from under a bed. Myrtle was dehydrated but in good spirits. We returned her, to the relief of all concerned, to the pond.

Next, without my knowing it, Lynn put tadpoles in the aquarium, and a week later we had to declare open season on bullfrogs throughout the house.

Shortly after this, our daughter began to concentrate on dogs. I succeeded housebreaking only one, a rat terrier named "Cricket".

There was a basset hound that really didn't mind "going" outdoors...if it happened to be there at the time. It felt the same way about the hall closet, the living room carpet and my bed.

But none of this equaled the 2 weeks we attempted to live with an antisocial skunk. It was not taken from the wild, but came originally from a pet store and was given to Lynn by a neighbor. At night (he neglected to tell us skunks sleep all day and roam about on search and destroy missions at night) it shredded all our magazines and swung gleefully from the dining room drapes.

It refused to sleep in the box we provided but collected tissue from the spindle in the bathroom and built a nest under the kitchen sink. Then it developed homicidal tendencies! It treed my mother-in-law on a chair, attacked Cricket every night at midnight and persistently gnawed on anyone willing to stand still. Exit the skunk.

There were more...many, many more. Like the hamster that lived in the piano, the possum that turned out to be harboring 13 smaller possums and the goat that broke down the kitchen door—on his way in.

But would I have it any other way? I love my children, and they love their pets. And though at the time I saw nothing remotely amusing about possum hunting in my underwear drawer, I will admit from the distance of a few years that it appears in a different light.

Besides, farm wives are blessed by nature with a slightly distorted sense of humor. How else could we survive?

Give Me a Normal 'Critter'

By Alana Phillips of Central Square, New York

No doubt about it—farming is a delightful endeavor…a wonderfully peaceful way to earn one's living.

The bite of the plow as it opens the earth. The feeling of accomplishment at the end of a long and fulfilling day. Homegrown and home-cooked everything leaking out of everywhere. And even if none of the above satisfactions existed, the mere aroma of fresh-cut hay alone would keep me down on the farm.

Yes, country life would be just about perfect if it weren't for one small inconvenience—the critters.

Now, don't get me wrong. My husband and I just adore those doe-eyed, placid cows that you see in all the dairy ads. (You know the type? The ones with the eyelashes down to their chins.) Or there are the cute little piglets who suck contentedly and immediately drift blissfully off to sleep. And the trusty 17 hands-high workhorse that even the 3-year-old can ride—it's gentle as a lamb yet can pull a fully loaded hay wagon 350 yds. straight uphill to the barn and then park it on a dime.

Nor can we forget the picture-perfect, ever-present barn cat and field dog. One quick and clever; the other faithful and diligent.

"In the entire time we had that cow, I found her up on my porch more often than the Avon lady!"

Right! On whose farm? Tell me where these paragons of country virtue reside, and I'll be there in a minute to purchase every last one of them to replace the misfits my husband and I seem to continually saddle ourselves with.

After 15 years of farming, he and I are convinced that "it must be something in the water". Every animal we add is perfectly normal when it arrives. But shortly thereafter a strange transformation takes place, and that gentle milk cow or reliable workhorse suddenly becomes a cross between "El Toro the Killer Bull" and "Tesoro the Mule Headed Donkey."

Currently residing here at the Phillips Funny Farm we have:

1. A dog who is too stupid to walk around the pond during the winter and consequently falls in with amazing regularity, necessitating a 100-yd. dash from the house by me, usually in bedroom

15

slippers, to drag her out.

2. A succession of cats who have conspired to turn the most awkward spot on the property into what seems like a continuous maternity ward. Given the opportunity, do these foolish felines opt for our abundant haymow or our luxurious sawdust bin? Of course not!

No spot on the ole' homestead seems to fulfill their peculiar requirements except the filthy, claustrophobic and totally inaccessible crawl space above the back room of our house. Their only means of access to this cat haven is literally to scale the side of a decrepit cinder-block chimney, and their sole exit is a monumental leap to the rafters some distance below!

But their perseverance never wavers. One distraught mother unfortunate enough to deliver outside the confines of the "Maternity Ward" promptly seized each of her small charges by the scruff

---

"Our serene horse sudddenly went berserk and ran through the fence—not once, but five times!"

---

of the neck and resolutely attacked that cinder-block bastion, not willing to rest until her entire brood was safely where she wanted them. Freezing in the winter, an inferno in the summer, and totally unsuitable all of the time, our crawl space has sheltered more litters than the local humane society.

3. We also have in residence a young horse who was so placid and well-behaved all the time we visited her that we almost didn't buy her.

"Not enough spirit," we said. "No gumption," we agreed.

So much for our horse sense. Within a week of her arrival she had managed to demolish two lengths of our pasture fence.

Being the experienced "horse people" that we are, we had spent an entire morning replacing every foot of barbed wire with smooth wire in preparation for letting the horse out. After admiring our handiwork for a few minutes, we escorted our calm, serene creature out into the pasture—where she immediately went berserk!

She didn't content herself with running through the fence just once. Oh no, not our horse! She went out one section of the fence, then back in another; out another and in a fourth. And as the coup de grace, out the last section that remained standing on that side, shearing off two 3-ft. wooden fence posts for good measure. Back she went to the barn...back we went to restring the fence.

4. And let us not forget our cow who thought she was housebroken. She had horns like a Brahma bull and feet like dinner plates. No small specimen, she. But she was easy to milk and not fussy about her feed. So far, so good, I mused. One normal animal out of the bunch isn't all bad.

Experience should definitely have taught me better than that. In the entire time that we had that cow, I found her up on my porch more often than the Avon lady. She was perfectly well behaved—the cow, not the Avon lady—and would readily agree to being led back to her pasture.

More often than not, however, by the time I had climbed back up the hill from the field, gotten into the house and removed my boots, there she was, front feet firmly planted on the porch. (That's all that would fit!) There she'd stand, content to gaze into the window by the hour as long as something was going on in the kitchen.

5. We've had pigs that I am certain must have been direct descendants of Harry Houdini. To keep them in, we had to nail their stall door shut with No. 16 nails. My *house* isn't even put together that well!

6. And we certainly can't slight our "wild ducks". Did they enjoy the beautiful, algae-covered, overgrown feast of a pond that we provided for them? Of course not. Every morning without fail we found them swimming and quacking to their heart's content in our neighbors' barren, boring, chemical-laden swimming pool.

Critters! you can't farm without 'em...and you can't farm with them!

The Coupon Caper

By Kathleen Willey of Port Orchard, Washington

It all started innocently enough. I chanced upon an article by a housewife who claimed she saved hundreds of dollars a year in groceries by shopping with coupons. She even went so far as to insist that often a $60 basket of groceries involved a cash outlay of just $5.

Suddenly I envisioned my supermarket actually paying me to shop! Coupons were, I decided emphatically, worth a fling. In my naivete and with the innocence born of ignorance, I honestly believed that I had nothing to lose.

I reread the article. Organization seemed to be the key—unfortunately, organization is a quality for which I've never been acclaimed. In fact, preparing meals so that meat and vegetables are done simultaneously is a skill that, so far, has eluded me.

"No matter, people can change," I muttered to myself as I made a quick list of the money-saving steps: **1.** Clip coupons. **2.** Save and file labels and packages as proof of purchase. **3.** Shop from a list. There, that looked *particularly* organized to me.

I was pleased to note that I already had a head start on my new shopping program. I've been making out shopping lists for years. Of course, the lists rarely get all the way to the store. Still it was a beginning.

That night over supper of meat a little too crisp and potatoes a trifle too chewy, I related my new plan to my family. My husband was skeptical, but he's a terrible cynic anyway. Our 14-year-old daughter, Jeanne, on the other hand, wasn't only enthusiastic, she volunteered for the coupon clipping and label filing.

In her adolescent enthusiasm she began clipping coupons immediately. I had to snatch from her nimble fingers a brand-new magazine, but not before she had mutilated the last page of a partly read mystery. Even with a few false starts, we soon had an impressive stack of coupons.

Finally the "test run" was upon me. I had the shopping list my daughter had taped to the outside of my purse and the coupon envelope tucked securely inside.

"The coupons are organized alphabetically," Jeanne assured me. "It's incredibly simple. Sure you don't want me to go with you?" She looked worried.

"No," I announced airily, "I rather prefer shopping alone; I'm more efficient that way."

I breezed confidently into the store and marched directly to the personal care section. I smiled brightly at other shoppers while I retrieved the coupon envelope from my purse. I looked under "s" for shampoo...and found three coupons for cat food. We don't even *have* a cat!

I rummaged in my purse for change and placed a hasty phone call home to my daughter. "I think you need to explain your system to me. I want shampoo."

"Look under "b" for bathroom," she said with the deep sigh annoyingly typical of a 14-year-old. "You'll find soap and toilet paper there, too."

The pulse fluttered in my right temple—a sure sign of a headache on its way.

"I know I shouldn't ask, but why cat food coupons? And why under 's'?"

Now she sounded absolutely vexed. "Mom, that stands for *someday*. Someday, if we get a cat, we'll need those coupons."

The flutter in my temple was definitely mutating into a genuine pain. "Gotcha," I said with false cheerfulness and hung up the phone.

The rest of the morning went in an anything but wonderful whirl. Soon coupons were stuffed in my pockets, scattered in the

---

"Somebody has taken the labels off all the cans!"

---

shopping basket or clenched in my teeth. My vision became blurred from acute label-readingitis.

Sometime during my second hour in the store I began flinging anything into the basket that had a coupon on the package. By now the headache had wrapped itself snugly around my skull. I returned to the drug counter and tossed an economy-sized bottle of aspirin into the basket, too.

Finally I stood at the checkout stand, removed the coupons from my teeth and handed them to the clerk. I felt almost revived and even a trifle smug. That sense of rising panic I usually experience as the groceries are tallied was missing. After all, I had coupons.

Then the total appeared...a good $20 more than I usually spend! I received 45¢ back on coupon refunds.

"Of course," I muttered to myself as I staggered to the car, "a plan is always more expensive in the beginning."

By the time I was safely home and Jeanne and I were putting

away the groceries, invisible little gnomes had begun pounding steel pins into my skull.

I opened the pantry door, and suddenly I could hear myself screeching, "Somebody has taken the labels off all the cans."

Jeanne's lower lip trembled. "I just wanted to get a head start on saving labels, Mom. You can still tell what's what. These are all soup cans, and these little cans here are either oysters or tomato sauce. And these have to be either tuna or clams."

"Give me those labels!" I managed to choke out from between clenched teeth. I wadded them and the coupons into a ball and chucked them in the trash can.

The gnomes suddenly ceased their pounding; I started smiling.

"This," I explained to my bewildered offspring, "may be the smartest thing I've ever done to preserve both my sanity and family harmony."

I studied the cans. They were quite attractive standing there wrapped in nothing but shiny aluminum.

"Okay, Jeanne," I said, "let's open one of those small cans for our lunch. We'll have either oyster stew or tomato sauce over something."

I may not be organized, but I *am* noted for my flexibility.

Exercises a la Lavon

By Lavon Baldauf Hoppes of Roca, Nebraska

We see them everywhere...those exercise fanatics, sweating their uncooperative bodies into whistleable figures. Farm women, you know, are no different than all those joggers, walkers, swimmers and aerobic devotees. We, too, want our husbands to come pulsing home to kiss our hands, bearing bushels of red roses and admiring our perfect figures.

But when it comes to fitting that half hour of television exercise into our morning or driving 20 miles to the nearest health club, the shapely image fades fast.

I confronted this shrinking dilemma, determined to find an exercise program fit for farm women. In no time, "Exercises a la Lavon" was born.

The first exercise used to be prefaced by "Open the gate, honey, please." Now my movements are automatic. When the pickup stops,

---

"Keep that tummy pulled in... or get it hit when the gate comes loose!"

I bail out and begin an exercise guaranteed to take off those fluffy mounds around the middle.

Equipment Needed: One gate.

Procedure: Run to the gate; inhale deeply. Now reach and stretch around the old gate post. Then stretch the other hand to pull the wire over the top. Up, up and off the post.

Keep that tummy pulled in—or get it hit when the gate comes loose. Now fast...drag the gate out of the way, pulling those lazy back muscles. Once hubby drives through, you can repeat this refreshing exercise sequence in reverse.

(You might encourage your husband to keep his gates and fences tightly stretched, as the exercise will be more strenuous and thus more beneficial.)

Now let's work on those flabby thighs. (Sometimes I wish I had the *chance* to get mine a little flabby.) This wonderful exercise will actually tighten you on every side—the front, the back and the middle, too.

Equipment Needed: One scoop.

Procedure: Grasp the tool tightly with both hands. Now bend at the waist ever so slightly. (Feel those greasy tummy muscles tighten?) Next push the scoop under a pile of grain, lift a full scoop and heave it into the truck. Keep up this rhythm of a scoop a second. Great, I tell you!

Let's not forget the hands! The main goal here is to produce hands with no wrinkles that look 20 years younger, like your daughter's.

Equipment Needed: A creature with four udder spigots.

Procedure: Chase and corral the creature for your cardiovascular workout. Flex the hands, position the bucket and begin opening and closing your hands with a squeezing action around the aforesaid spigots.

If some of the milk is spilled by a well-placed kick, you have the added advantage of a milk bath—always good for the complexion. Come summer, this exercise is a tremendous way of getting your neck in shape as you repeatedly dodge that vicious tail searching for pesky flies. You can combine this with a lot of fast "toe touches" as you avoid that flying hind leg.

My "Exercises a la Lavon" program offers much more, too. I might mention posthole digging for a terrific up and down shaper-upper...or riding old "Pal" in the roundup all day—it's sure to jiggle pounds away.

Now in the house, scrubbing, ironing, sweeping, carrying wet wash up the stairs, out to the clothesline and back in, ironed clothes up the stairs and clothes to be laundered down, toting food and dishes down to the kids in the rec room and the dirty dishes up to the kitchen—these all aid farm women in their quest for *the* perfect figure.

To benefit fully, though, "Exercises a la Lavon" should be done 3 times a week—at a minimum. But just in case your farm or ranch doesn't have the needed equipment, come on over, I'll supply everything...including the jobs...to turn your figure into a sleek machine. And you won't have to worry, develop wrinkles or seek an analyst for your frustrations either!

The Hog and I

By Beth Joiner of Tennille, Georgia

I t's 3 a.m. Do you know where your husband is? I roll over in bed, throw my arm out but no one's there. Instantly I know where my husband is.

Not for him the sophisticated curves of a movie star. No, he prefers the round "American beauty" called the hog. And whether it's a cold December morning or a hot June afternoon, he's by her side when she is having pigs.

There were some skeptics who wagged their fingers and clucked their tongues when Benjie and I married, saying that a dancing teacher and a hog farmer would hardly be a compatible combination. And there have been times when I was tempted to believe them!

But for a city girl who had never personally met a hog, couldn't tell a cow from a horse and didn't know soybeans from cotton, I haven't done too badly. I can now drive most any tractor, herd hogs, converse fairly intelligently on the size of pork chops and steel myself to remain in the hog house, ripe with pungent odor, for at least 5 minutes. That may not sound like much to someone who calls herself a seasoned farmer, but I challenge any city slicker to beat my record.

The majority of the time, Benjie and I have managed pretty well during my "education". I forgave him when he accidentally innoculated me for lepto (I wasn't really doing a good job of holding the squealing, wriggling pig), and he forgave me for the time I scratched my nose at a hog sale and bought a $2,000 boar.

But harmony is halted every now and then. One such incident came early in our marriage when Benjie couldn't decide between "the hog" and me.

As it happened, a purebred sow was due to farrow about the same time that I was...that is, she was about to have pigs—and I was about to have our first baby! It had been enough to have Benjie refer to our condition on a regular basis in the same terms, for I considered myself a notch or two above the hog. But this was a special sow, mind you, one that might produce a future champion that could sell for perhaps $20,000...a far cry from what my husband expected me to produce. He clearly felt that he might have to spend $20,000 over the first 5 years of our child's life.

For a few weeks he wavered back and forth between the hog and me, remaining in a constant state of indecision over which of us would receive his attention. The sow came to my rescue, however, and delivered 10 squealing piglets 3 days before our common due

25

date. I silently thanked her.

Though that situation with the sow was solved easily, there have been other times when things have not been so simple. Heaven help Benjie if he ever again names a pig "Big Red Beth"!

"Now that is a pretty pig," my husband said one night as he looked through the *Duroc Journal*.

"Let me see," I asked. My husband pointed to a stout red hog with her nose in a feed dish.

"That's nice," I said loyally while not really understanding what I was looking at.

"Now pay attention," my husband, the frustrated teacher, said. "I'm going to show you how to pick out the best hogs. Then when I go to hog sales, you can help me buy."

"All right," I said agreeably, and he launched into a 10-minute lecture that went right over my head.

"Now pick out the worst boar on this page," Benjie said as he covered up the captions beneath the pictures. I was supposed to put my newly gained knowledge to work and study the size of those hams, the bone structure and the amount of backfat. I stared intensely at the pictures for perhaps a minute, but no matter how hard I looked I couldn't find any differences.

"There, that one," I finally said when I found a hog that was standing at an odd angle with his back all hunched up. That surely had to be the worst hog.

"Oh, Beth," my husband said with a grimace, "that is the grand champion boar from the Southeastern Conference. I don't believe you heard a word I said."

"Yes, I did," I replied, and I had. But I am a firm believer that you have to have a knack for these things, and I just don't have it.

But, on the whole, the "hog" and I have gotten along fairly well over the past few years. Just please—no more "Beths" as my "competition"!

Driveway Desperation!

By Lucie Stigler of Buckeystown, Maryland

My motto has always been, "Let well enough alone". I can eye a crooked fence row and think "picturesque" instead of "needs fixin' ". The "bit rough" edges around our farm don't tug at my conscience. I've even managed at times to carry my "all's well" optimism over to our mile-long driveway...although it's caused me hours of anguish.

For the longest time I thought it possessed its own farm charm. To live with it, I simply navigated around the potholes, dips and gullies!

I must admit, though, that my ton truck has never done as well. I often bounce high enough to hit my head on the cab roof with such force that I have to stop to collect my wits. But my pickup does just fine, although I do replace shock absorbers often. And in my car—I can weave a snappy zigzag route. On horse, I have no problems at all!

Our guests, however, have often become "unstuck" after driving into our farm. Some are ashen on arrival...some look beneath

---

"I hit the halfway mark and slid deep into a snowdrift—stopped cold, so to speak!"

---

their cars...men frequently give a mighty kick to tires, although that maneuver could make things worse, it seems to me. But men will be men and kick tires. Women are a bit tousled, and it's a moment before they speak.

After several such instances when husband Aug and I thought we were losing all our friends, I dropped my "well-enough-alone" attitude and took action against the driveway.

"Your birthday gift is here," I chirped to Aug one day as I eyed the mammoth gravel truck pulling in.

"You didn't buy me a truck!" Aug exclaimed, hurrying out.

"No, just some No. 2 crusher-run gravel," I commented as he began to spread his gift around.

But that gravel was soon digested and consumed by holes turned craters. So why not big stuff, I thought? The next year I ordered 3-in. gravel instead. Aug wasn't around, so our hired hand did the spreading...or was it heaving? He looked absolutely done in when the empty truck pulled away, and Aug looked absolutely stricken when he saw the results.

"That stuff's too big. It's rocks with pointed..." he began. After a couple slashed tires, I agreed and returned to crusher-run gravel.

Of course, that doesn't help in the winter, the worst of times drivewaywise. Wind piles snow on top of our scenic drive like icing on a cake. A 3-in. snowfall can produce 3-ft. drifts, defying all the laws of nature!

One winter it was my lot to pick up some tractor parts on a wind-slamming day—after the driveway had been "cleared", Aug assured me. I headed out in the car and hit the halfway mark. At that point I slid deep into a drift and was stopped cold, so to speak.

Undaunted, I walked back to the barn and started the pickup, deciding to cross the snow-strewn field and skirt the lane completely.

I bounced over the rolling field, spiked with cornstalks. Suddenly that pickup slid into a spot with no stalks and sank low...seemingly permanently. Once again I trudged home!

Surely the big truck could make it, I thought with more determination than intelligence. I climbed aboard, drove in the first set

---

"Winter turned to spring—and the driveway was inundated with holes, pools, streams, ponds and small lakes..."

---

of tracks, rather cleverly zigged out into the field around the stuck car and back into the lane—where I came to a tire-spinning halt.

The walk home this time was longer, and my toes, already wet from two earlier treks, were frozen together. Now out of wheels, I stayed put, dreading the towing operation—and that infamous "I told you so" look from Aug—that I knew would come all too soon.

Just before dark he stalked in. "I could have made it in, but the lane is blocked...and what is the truck doing in the field...and how did they *all* get stuck?"

My explanation was lost in the winds and sleet that bombarded us as we headed out with chains and tractor. One at a time the trucks and car came home. At the end I examined my toes for any signs of life, wondering at their strange coloration and tingle.

That winter had done its worst, and soon spring arrived with a deluge of rains. Holes, pools, streams, ponds and small lakes inundated the driveway. Birthday time rolled around again, and I inquired—about blacktop prices. Then I ordered *more* crusher-run!

One watery day—with dinner waiting—elderly relatives came

to visit. The lady hurried in, but her husband stayed behind the steering wheel, the car's motor running. His face was a study in terror. Seems they couldn't be staying, she rambled.

"He hit one of those holes and heard a crack somewhere underneath," she reported, voice shaking. "Something vital must be broken. He's afraid to turn off the motor...it may not start again!"

In truth, his car sounded terminal and—our mud dripping from it didn't look so good either. I fixed a care package as apology for that "awful lane", and they threaded their way back to safety. (We learned later that the diagnosis was accurate. The engine was frozen to something or other and required major surgery. They never visited again!)

"Aug, we *must* do something about that driveway!" I finally announced, completely abandoning my "let-well-enough-alone" attitude. "We can cope, but..." We agreed to the expenditure of blacktop all the way along.

But another winter came and went, and when spring arrived with all its demands, we invested all ready cash in a bigger tractor. (Easier to clear and grade the driveway, we figured.) But we did resolve that next year, *for sure* we'll blacktop. I just wonder if we'll have any friends left when we do!

Life With Renoir

By Doris Bircham of Piapot, Saskatchewan

You've got paint dripping off your elbow again!" my husband shouts from the top of his ladder.

"So what?" I retort, glancing down at a spotted white trail leading across the lawn to where I'm standing, painting the house. How can a man who has one of the untidiest workshops in the country be such a fanatic about painting, I wonder.

When we built our new house a few years ago, he carefully undercoated each wall then sanded the entire thing, ceilings and all—to remove fine hairs, he said. Two, sometimes three coats of paint were artfully applied to each room. I looked on, content in the knowledge that I might have one of the few hairless wallboard houses known to man.

I really do try to be careful. But somehow the paint always ends up in the base of the bristles, running down the brush handle and my arm. My husband, on the other hand, dips his brush in an

---

"I could have broken two legs and my elbow, but my husband was bemoaning the half gallon of red paint spattered in the dirt!"

---

inch or two, gets rid of excess paint on the underside lip of the can and glides away with smooth, even strokes.

It's the brushing that makes the paint job, he tells me. If I mention the virtues of paint sprayers and rollers, he stares at me with that same look I got when I told him one of the bulls had broken into the heifer field.

He looks on in horror when I grease myself—face included—with hand cleaner, don sunglasses to keep the paint out of my eyes, bundle up like an Eskimo and go to work. I sometimes forget to stir the paint thoroughly, or worse still stir in bits of skin that have settled on top of the paint and then neglect to strain the whole mess.

Once I failed to keep the main container covered and had to plead guilty to a scum of dust, colored leaves and wriggling bugs. And I always get the top rim of the can full of paint so when I replace the lid, paint squirts out in all directions. I've also known to slop paint down the printed side of the can so the instructions and paint lot numbers are obliterated forever.

Lately I've taken to pouring small amounts of paint into ice cream buckets. That technique came about after a ladder wreck when we were painting our barn and quonset. I could have broken two legs and my elbow, but my husband was bemoaning the half gallon of red paint spattered in the dirt. That same day some folks dropped by and commented on the unusual color of our border collie (black and white with "ranch red" markings).

Another time we had almost finished painting the outside of our house when my husband had to be away for a few days. On Sunday the weather was ideal for painting so I decided to surprise him by finishing the trim. I dressed for the job in a three-sizes-too large ragged shirt and a pancake-style cap pulled down to the top of my sunglasses.

By 4 p.m. I had finished the last gable end and the trim around two windows on the north side of our house in dark forest green. Proudly I stood back, noting there was hardly a spatter on the white wall below.

Although the sky had been cloudless all day, an hour after I finished one of those torrential thunderstorms that pop up out of

---

"I dream of buildings made of brick, stucco, stainless steel or stone!"

---

nowhere struck. It pounded against my north wall, then vanished as quickly as it came...but not without leaving its mark. My wall had a tie-dyed look, with wavy shades of green veering in all directions across the white. Several buckets of hot water and cleaner later I retreated, exhausted, back inside the house. I've never painted on a Sunday since.

Sometimes I think my husband is becoming fussier, but it could have something to do with the high cost of paint these days. Today under his watchful eye, I finish these last two boards, and as I work I dream of buildings made of brick, stucco, stainless steel or stone.

Who knows, maybe by next year some manufacturer will develop a fantastic paint that will be instant-on, come in a light disposable container and carry a minimum guarantee of 75 years.

Load 'Em Up! Head 'Em Out!

By Frieda Brockman of Esther, Alberta

Being married to a farmer puts me in the precarious position of sharing the unique brand of excitement his occupation involves. Not that I've ever complained that my life's boring—how could it be on a farm? It's just that "thrills" seem to come with the territory.

I can always expect a stimulating morning when I hear, "I'm taking the bull to the community pasture today. You'll have to help load him" from my farmer, Rob, over the breakfast table.

Now, raising cattle for market may be the farmer's bread and butter. Loading them, however, is what puts the spice in his diet.

"I'm scared stiff of that bull!" I exclaim.

But do my fears matter? Soon I find myself on the end of a rope just in front of Rob with that snorting beast on the other end.

"He doesn't like me," I hiss. "As soon as he sees me, he snorts and paws like that."

"Don't be silly!" Rob answers in a tone that sounds as if I'd made a sacrilegious remark.

Rob gives a masterful tug on the rope. And on cue, "Bully" takes the stage as if this is his shining hour and he's giving us a little preview of the national rodeo finals.

With a single snort, he heads straight for the old swing pole. The sudden jerk throws us into a forward dive with such force we

---

"Loading cattle is a job best done without the help of the family pet, especially if it happens to be our dog 'Rover'."

---

barely maintain our footing. We hang on though, like bulldogs with a beef steak. I figure that the end of the lariat is as safe a place as any, at least while Rob is in the middle.

Near the swing pole, that 2,000 lbs. of meanness stops, snorts and paws the ground. Rob takes advantage of the lull and winds the rope around the pole several times.

"I don't know what's gotten into him," Rob gasps.

"I keep telling you, he doesn't like me!" I inform him again.

At the sound of my voice, the bull lowers his head, gives a bellow and charges at us.

33

"Look out!" I scream. At the same instant, Rob and I take off as if we've been catapulted off an aircraft carrier. For a time or two around the pole it's difficult to tell who's chasing whom. Then I veer off in the direction of the house without a backward glance.

Rob leaves the bull tied to the post for a couple of hours, giving him time to calm down. Then he loads him by simply leading him up the chute. He doesn't ask me to help.

"That bull just walked right up. Something must have spooked him this morning...or maybe he really doesn't like you," Rob chuckles afterward.

I could live peacefully if our farm's flair for excitement ended there. But there was a black steer who gave me the runaround, too. That critter was a better escape artist than Houdini.

Every time we had a load of cattle to take to market, we vowed it would be the steer's turn to join them. Again and again, however, "Supersteer" would leap high corrals at a single bound to avoid his fate.

"I'll bet that steer will be on this place until he dies of old age," I complained to Rob after the animal had made another of his vaults to freedom just when we thought we had him on his way.

Finally Rob, with some trickery and an exceptional streak of luck, loaded the steer directly out of the barn onto the truck. The last I saw of him, he had his front feet up on the stock racks as Rob drove past the house.

"If he'd had just an inch more room in that truck box, he'd have cleared the racks," Rob told me later.

Taking a heifer and her calf to market provided yet another inauspicious loading event. We had just opened the barn door and let them into the corral when our dog, "Rover", appeared on the scene. (Loading cattle, we've found, is a job best done without the help of the family pet, *especially* Rover.) The heifer was skittish and nervously possessive of her calf.

Rover was no dummy in his choice of opponents. He danced around the calf, making surly noises. Suddenly the heifer lunged at Rover, who immediately took refuge behind me. I took refuge up the side of the corral.

"Where did that coward disappear to?" I screamed from my perch on the top rail.

Rover had vanished, the heifer was inspecting her baby, and Rob was standing at the barn door with his mouth open.

I might be able to live with these "trials by fire" if our working conditions were fit for humans. But our cattle loading often takes place just after a rain, since we can't do any other work then. It's not my favorite job even when the corrals are dry, but I don my son's rubber boots. (They're at least 2 sizes too big—mine are usually missing when I need them.)

For an hour or so, I stomp around the corral. By then my boots have taken on so much mud they resemble pontoons.

"Feet like this should only belong to Paul Bunyan," I told Rob once.

"Don't let that steer out," he shouted back, paying no attention to my words or the size of my feet.

Just then the speckle-faced critter darted off at a 90° angle, leaving me in the wake of a spray of mud and slush. By the time the animal was loaded, much more than my feet was caked with mud.

Some people, I've concluded, lead an exciting life by doing death-defying stunts, acrobatics, knife throwing or putting out oil well fires. But the farmer has his own insurance against boredom.

He just backs his truck up to the loading chute and calls his wife—then the action really begins!

Farmish...Is It Anything Like English?

BY DIANA STOUT HOFFMAN OF MARSHALL, MICHIGAN

Farmers speak a whole different language. For those of us who speak English, it sometimes takes a while to understand them—but if you press them hard enough, I've learned, everything eventually makes sense.

For example, the other day my husband and I were returning from a dairy luncheon when I noticed we were headed in the opposite direction from the farm.

"Why are we going this way? Marshall's back there," I said to him while pointing behind me.

"Thought I'd take a shortcut through Concord (a neighboring community)," he replied.

"How do you figure it's a shortcut when we're going 2 miles out of our way?" I asked.

"Think of the miles and gas I'm saving by not going home just to come back to take a look at Concord," he replied.

"You'd come all the way back here? Just to look at Concord?"

"There isn't a farmer alive who isn't able to sniff out an implement dealership within a 5-mile radius!"

I questioned, feeling positively puzzled but not about to drop the subject. "What's in Concord?"

"Uh...uh...what do you mean what's in Concord?" he said innocently.

"Just that—what's in Concord?" I had my suspicions, but I wanted to hear it from him.

"An implement dealer," he mumbled.

"Ah-ha!" I cried. The truth was out!

There isn't a farmer alive who isn't able to sniff out a dealership within a 5-mile radius. They'll drive for 2 hours in circles sure that it's there somewhere. It has to be—it was there 20 years ago when they were in the area for a farm auction.

That in turn allows you to hear what they bought that many

years ago. They'll excitedly point out the farm, tell you how much more they paid for the machine than they should have and how sorry they still are they didn't buy that manure spreader that was for sale that day, too.

About the time you have a headache, they spot the dealership and brake down to 10 miles an hour on a main highway so they can get a good look at the machinery, deciding whether it's worth stopping for a closer inspection. This in turn catches unprepared drivers behind you off guard...how are they to know they're following a farmer who brakes at each and every piece of machinery?

Next you find yourself sitting in the car watching this man-child romp between those monstrous work horses as he notes prices

---

"I'm training my farmer to mean he'll be home in an hour when he says an hour... instead of arriving after 3 have passed."

---

and looks up into engines, all the while unaware of icy puddles, 50 mph wind and near blizzard.

As for language...a much misunderstood term spoken by the keeper of the cows is "going for a drive". A farmer's wife must never *ever* believe her husband is offering to take her for a leisurely Sunday drive, especially when it's during the middle of the week on a sunny day.

Still...hoping against hope some miracle has taken place in my husband's unromantic heart, I'll always agree, only to find us driving slow enough to require an orange triangle on the back of our truck. No farmer can resist a bimonthly trip to the fields in the spring to see if the rows are straight and the ground is becoming Irish in color.

In vain I've tried to help my farmer speak English. I'm training him to mean he'll be home in an hour when he says an hour, instead of arriving after 3 have passed. Or when he says I'll do it tomorrow, which in most people's language means the next day, not to mean a week from next Thursday.

On the other hand, if his language is relearned, I might miss hearing him say, "Hurry, hurry, come out here quick!" Rushing out expecting to see blood on someone, I'll find him looking at the sky watching a triangle of Canada geese flying home or a sunset bathed in pastels.

Maybe I ought to reconsider this language barrier. Maybe there's something to be said for speaking "farmish".

Is There Life After The Well Goes Dry?

BY JOYCE WHITIS OF STEPHENVILLE, TEXAS

Have you ever climbed into the shower after a hot, tiring day, turned on the water, soaped your body, worked shampoo into your hair—then watched in horror as the stinging spray from the nozzle turns to a trickle...then a drip...then nothing?

Now suppose that in the final seconds before the water stopped altogether, muddy water spewed out of the shower head. Being totally unprepared for any of this—and covered with soap, shampoo and mud to boot—might bring on hysteria. At least it did with *me*.

When my practical husband, Tom, finally got me calmed down, he said, "Well, I guess I'd better call somebody to fix the well."

"Fix the well! How about me? Who's going to fix me? I feel like I've been scrubbed down with sandpaper and left out to dry...to say nothing about the syrup in my hair!"

Undaunted, he directed me to our son's house, just down the road, where a well pumped clear water in a refreshing surge through pipes showing no signs of disintegration. I retreated to there, wrapped in towels and robe. But not before catching the attention of all the dogs in the yard.

As I paraded toward the car, they jumped to attention. "Atilla" caught hold of my left arm in his giant jaw and spun me around so he could look into my mud-streaked face. His puzzled eyes studied the pitiful sight I had become, and then he let go of my arm to spit out some of the sand caught between his teeth. At that moment, I bolted to the car.

Sometime later, clean and fluff-dried, I felt better able to handle our waterless house. But surely I couldn't be expected to cook without water! So to town we went to supper. By the time I had finished my steak, I was ready to face the disaster.

Getting somebody to drill a new well was harder than living without water, I learned. I spent a lot of time on the phone talking to folks whose business is drilling wells. The first one told me it would probably be 6 weeks.

"Six weeks!" I screamed. "The deodorant and cologne won't hold out that long."

The second driller said it would be 2 months. The next two never returned my calls. Finally I found a man in the next town who promised to be here in 5 days.

We discovered as we waited that when forced to we could get by on a surprisingly small amount of water. Tom filled two milk cans every morning at the dairy, and we left them in the back of the pickup parked in the sun all day.

Solar energy heated the water inside the cans so at bath time the temperature was exactly right—right for stepping out behind the house to bathe and brush our teeth, that is. Out of necessity we waited until after dark for this, but I'll tell you there's something lovely about a soapy, refreshing bath under the stars. And once more I gave thanks for the privacy of country living.

Other normal tasks were manageable, too. We heated water on the stove for dishwashing—just like in the good old days—and watered plants with leftover face-washing water.

I know this all may sound a lot like a Pollyanna tale, but it's true...being without running water can be endured, even fun at times. Of course, I have to confess—when I saw the well driller pull his rig into our lane, I ran out and hugged his feet!

Throwing in the Towel

By Mary A. Morman, Rochester, Minnesota

I am throwing in the towel. Literally. These are no figurative words signifying the end of a marriage or a friendship, nor capitulation in the Madison Square Garden sense. I'm deliberately tossing an honest-to-goodness terry cloth bath variety into the washer and dryer.

I gave in to dirt long ago. As children's footsteps crossed our threshold bringing half of the pasture in day after day, my protests weakened. I settled for quick wipes at the tracks and handprints. Still I drew the line at baths and dirty clothes...until somewhere along the way the kids and I switched sides and I started saying, "Please, do you have to be *that* clean?"

I'd always accepted laundering as a daily chore, but things started to get out of hand when my son, reaching 11-1/2, discovered girls, shampoo, deodorant and the 6 a.m. shower all at the same time. Arriving for breakfast—shampooed, scrubbed and fresh laundry-scented—he deepened my maternal pride.

What were a few extra towels, I thought. Even ones abandoned to mildew on the bathroom floor or others wadded in damp clumps beside his bed I considered progress. So he was sloppy. He'd outgrow it. Wouldn't he?

Instead, he just grew...as did my young daughter—*and* my terry travail.

"She's not a greasy sleaze anymore," observed wise, sarcastic and still very clean Older Brother, now aged 13. Indeed, no more

---

"Showering requires at least three towels per person: one for the hair, one for the body (two if the bathroom's cold) and one for the feet!"

"greasies" for 10-year-old Little Sister, who used to spend more time on grooming her pony than she did herself.

"Feathered" as in Farrah Fawcett was fading slowly, too slowly, in the Midwest. Accordingly, early morning shampoos, blow-drying and "feathering" with the curling iron took precedence over a family institution: Mom's mandatory, nutritious breakfast.

To be sure, clean curls are an improvement over dank locks; therefore, I generously praised Susan's lustrous coiffure but privately

41

lamented the missed or abbreviated breakfasts...as well as the growing number of towels she used.

I knew we had reached a crisis the morning I counted 19 used towels in the bathroom. Immediately—if cautiously—I laid out the problem.

"Kids, we've got Towel Trouble with a capital T," I said tentatively, not wanting them to think I did not whole-heartedly approve of bathing. In the discussion that followed, I learned:

a) Showering requires at least three towels per person: one for the hair, one for the body (two if the bathroom is cold) and one more for the feet.

b) Towels are dropped on the floor because there isn't time to hang them; moreover, the towel racks are always full, especially when *some* people shower more than once daily.

c) There is an adolescent axiom, as yet unnamed, which governs consumption of bath towels *and* laundered blue jeans, canned

---

"In despair I calculated how many towels I'd launder before they entered college or left home!"

---

pop, snack foods, hot water and electricity. Stated plainly, it says: "We got plenty, so why not?"

d) Towels are *never* reused. What if somebody mistakenly used another person's? Horror of horrors! There could be a leper in the family.

Their logic and argumentative abilities were superior to mine. To my 20-odd reasons why they should reform in the bathroom, they had 26 rebuttals. I gave up. I had no answers, but my older-and-wiser neighbor down the road, with three children in college, did.

"Refold the dried, used towels and put them back in the linen closet," Shirley advised. "They take three baths a day, so who has germs?"

Brilliant! For a few weeks I carefully spread the towels to dry, later folding them for reuse. I smiled slyly some mornings when I heard the linen closet door slam, confident I was as clever as Shirley.

Success was brief! "Mom, why is this towel stiff and boardy?" asked the next Miss Clairol. "Didn't you use softener?"

"I'm out," I lied. So much for that idea. Besides I'd begun to worry about Great-Aunt Grace's upcoming annual visit. What if I gave her a recycled towel? My mother and countless other relatives, probably all of southeast Missouri, would know, that's what!

Shopping the white sales, I found another solution. I bought dark blue towels for Son, light blue for Daughter and white for myself. No symbolism implied; only I know better not to step on white towels with muddy feet.

Pleased with my plushy towels in colors harmonizing with the bathroom wallpaper, I was inspired to monogram appropriate initials in pewter gray in the lower-right corner of each one. With continuing enthusiasm, I reorganized the linen closet while the towels laundered.

With the new towels stacked in place, the closet looked magazine picture-perfect. Smugly, I caressed the luxurious velour and counted the minutes until the school bus arrived.

As soon as the kids had devoured their after-school snacks, I ushered them upstairs. I displayed the tidied closet and told them I'd removed all the Snoopy, Star Wars, Hulk and assorted purple, green and orange flowered towels. "We now have a system," I explained. "Each person has new, color-coded personalized towels, to be *reused* at least twice before discarding."

Two sets of dark brown eyes flashed resentment. "But, Mom, I like my Darth Vader towel, and I'd rather have light blue than navy," asserted my son.

"Why can't I keep my Smiley Face towels?" implored my child with "feathered" tresses.

Firmly I announced, "Old towels are on the lower shelf, to be used *only* for Duchess' baths or for your trips to the pond." (Only 67% of the towels used for swimming ever return home, but that is another story.)

"Gol, Mom, if you say so," they finally assented, "we'll try."

Maybe they did. That the system worked beautifully for a few weeks is cause for wonder; that it soon fell apart is no surprise.

"He draped his wet towel on mine and polluted it"..."There are no more navy blue towels; I used mine to wipe out the backseat of the car when Dad and I brought that ewe and her lamb in from the pasture"..."Sorry, Mom, I forgot and used my towels to wash the dog last night"..."The dog was sick on my towel!"

In despair I calculated how many towels I'd launder before they entered college or left home (they will, won't they?). It gave me a migraine. So now I'm just throwing in the towel—towel after towel after towel...

My Honey's Bees!

BY HELEN ROSE PAULS OF LANGLEY, BRITISH COLUMBIA

Since our first year together, I had encouraged my hardworking mate to find a hobby, something good for mind and spirit, over and above the demands of daily farming. But each idea I suggested fell by the wayside, riddled with his excuses. It seemed that work, work, work would win out.

Then one bright day in early spring he strolled in to announce that he had found his hobby. A great smile rounded his square face in anticipation of my reaction.

"A hobby?" I shouted. "What is it?"

"Bees," he said. "Ten hives, all put together...except for two of them. The neighbor down the road is selling them all...to me! He's even throwing in the extractor."

"Throwing in the extractor, yet," I mumbled to myself in disbelief. But to him I said, "Hooray, you found your hobby!"

Then, on second thought, I added, "Just remember, it's all yours. I refuse to get involved."

"There's nothing to it," he replied. "Just a few hours a week checking the little workers as they bring in the honey. It's all in this manual!"

Soon 10 white columns stood impressively along the back fence. Neighbors began putting in orders for honey even before the wild flower season, and the bee hat and veil, elbow-length gloves and white coveralls suited hubby well.

Spring opened her leaves and flowers to summer, and a warm sun made the bees busier than ever. Always singly they would fly high, level off near our house, then dive-bomb onto the hive's threshold, where drones relieved them of their sweet load. The warm weather turned my mate as busy as the bees, and somehow he never found time to assemble the remaining two hives. Soon he would need the 10 supers to put on the other hives as they filled with honey; it was the bees only way of expansion.

"Here, I'll show you," he finally said one day before rushing to the field. "There's nothing to it. Join these two pieces with tacks, then these two. Draw wire through the holes, insert the undrawn comb, and you have a frame. Twelve frames make a super; five supers stacked up make a hive; paint them white and—voila! Two more hives to be used as needed."

Hating to see the equipment unused, my frugal nature won out, and I agreed to help—just this *once*. Many long afternoons later, the hives were ready for use and stood beside the others.

The bees maintained themselves for the rest of the summer, and frost time came quickly.

"Got to get that honey out, honey, before the bees get it all," he remarked, *often.*

But there was never time for that as another harvest took up my honey's days. So the bees stayed inside, and they, not we, enjoyed the honey.

Finally I relented again, allowing him to stack the full supers in one corner of the kitchen, just until he had time to extract them. Anything, I decided, to get them closer to the extractor. And there they sat, seeping honey and taking up space while work, work, work won out.

Orders for fresh honey piled up, and our impatient friends found honey elsewhere. Finally I timidly asked, "How does this thing

---

*"Honey dripped everywhere...
on me...on the floor. Whenever I walked, my
shoes stuck—psst, psst, psst—to the floor.*

---

work anyway?" Lifting the lid of the extractor, I peered inside.

"Oh, nothing to it at all," hubby replied on his way out the door to repair a combine. "Just melt off the wax on the frame with a hot knife, slide four frames into the extractor like this, close the lid, press the button and presto—honey!"

"Well, I'll just do enough for Fran and Darlene," I sighed.

Honey dripped everywhere. On me...on the floor. Whenever I walked, my shoes stuck—psst, psst, psst—to the floor.

Exactly 164 lbs. later and 18 supers left to go, I rested for the night. *Nothing* to this? I questioned.

It was 1 lb. for the mailman at Christmas; 1 for the baby-sitter's mother for helping her be so punctual; another for the neighbor who made oven mitts for Christmas for me; 25 lbs. to my brother for the loan of his car. Bartering worked!

"What happened to all that honey?" my honey asked one night at dinner.

"Oh, it's here and there. Lots more in the supers downstairs," I said.

"Tomorrow we'll finish it," he said.

"Right on!" I replied, then dared to ask, "By the way...how many hives are we getting *next* year?"

My Husband Went Haywire

BY LANA ROBINSON OF CRANFILLS GAP, TEXAS

Do you ever wonder how life on the farm might have been had some genius failed to invent baling wire? I've concluded that we might actually have had hinges and locks on our gates! Though the many wonders of this simple wire amaze me, my husband is fanatical about it.

The fact that baling wire binds hay into neat little bundles is secondary to my Melvin. This man has discovered 1,001 clever uses over the years, among them fence-mending, makeshift car antennas and tying up dragging mufflers. He also recently repaired a sagging fireplace screen with this miracle wire.

However, we experienced a family crisis not long ago that left me confused. It seems Melvin fell victim to a strange delusion... somehow he became convinced that baling wire is nearing extinction.

I first learned of his fear when he suggested we spend our family outings salvaging scraps of wire from abandoned farmsteads.

"But, honey," I reasoned, "the back of your truck has an infinite supply of baling wire."

"Yeah, Dad," our teenage son, Eric, chided. "We could collect aluminum cans if we were interested in wasting our weekends doing something really dumb. At least we'd make a few bucks."

Melvin winced. "You two don't understand. Conservation is essential. If we don't preserve the existing wire, future generations of farmers won't have any!"

This marked the beginning of his obsession with baling wire. While others were concerned with famine, poverty, wars and oppressed peoples, my husband was consumed with being prepared for the soon-to-be world shortage of baling wire. He ranted. He raved. He preached.

My concerns grew as fast as Melvin's stockpile. I decided it was time to seek professional help.

"Granny," I sobbed, pouring my heart out over the phone, "you were married to a farmer for almost 50 years. Please tell me what to do!"

"It'll pass, dear. Don't you fret," she assured me. "I remember this notion Herbert had once...he was dead-set against electric milkers. He feared those cold, impersonal machines would cause emotional disturbances in cows."

"Are you kidding me?" I sniffed.

"Nope," she chuckled. "He was afraid milk production would

drop. Imagine, he was one of the last dairymen in these parts to get electric milkers. He took an awful ribbing when he did."

Her counsel really helped, and my new found patience for Melvin's mania endured for all of 2 weeks.

"He's gone too far this time, Mom," Eric said, spilling his sad story. "He's trying to work a trade...our filly for four rolls of wire!

"Dad has literally gone haywire," he continued. "We've got to create a diversion of some kind...jolt him out of this madness!"

Diversion! Perhaps that was the answer. I fished my slinky red negligee out of mothballs and plotted my strategy...his favorite meat loaf, scented candles, soft music.

Early in the evening, I realized my plan was not going to be as simple as I thought. Melvin seemed preoccupied. After dinner, he retreated with the newspaper while I cleared the table and pondered my next move.

"Something bothering you?" I asked when he reappeared.

"I've been thinking," he said, helping himself to a second piece of coconut cream pie. "There's lots of talk about Central and South American countries falling to hostile governments."

"So?" For the life of me, I couldn't begin to guess where this conversation was leading.

He cleared his throat and assumed a reverent tone. "It comes a time in a man's life when he has to make a choice...a sacrifice..."

I whirled around. "You're not thinking of...?"

"Of course not," he replied. "It's just that Buford Worley is trying to make a deal to trade me 65 used tires for my wire."

I collapsed into the closest chair, certain my husband's jar was shy a pickle or two. "I'm afraid to ask...what does Buford plan to do with all that wire?"

Melvin cocked his head as if I'd asked a ridiculous question. "Same as me. When I shared my theory with him, he was in total agreement. He's a man of real conviction."

"Am I supposed to see some correlation between this and South America?"

"No, hon," he shook his head. "The connection is between the tires and South America."

This man is either a genius or insane, I thought.

"Don't you see? There's no telling where all this will stop," he whispered. "All those countries may be overrun and the rubber plantations lost! We'll be in real trouble...no rubber, no tires."

"And the sacrifice?" I was still trying to assemble all the bits and pieces into a reasonable line of thought.

"My wire collection, of course. Only the way I see it, it really

48

won't be much of a sacrifice if Buford will carry on where I left off. I feel he is trustworthy, a good steward toward his commitment. Knowing he will be faithful to the task will allow me to concentrate my efforts on saving rubber." A lofty, mystical expression captured his face.

Suddenly, the back door squeaked, and Eric walked in. Melvin draped an arm over our son's shoulder. "I'm glad you're home. I've got some exciting news to discuss with you."

Eric lagged behind as Melvin headed toward the den. "Mom, please tell me you thought of a diversion! Please tell me I won't have to sit through another sermon on baling wire!"

"Okay," I consoled him. "You won't have to sit through another sermon on baling wire."

"Then what's the news?"

"Well, son," I sighed, "it's good news and bad news. The good news is your father is no longer a baling wire tycoon." I squeezed him close. "Now for the bad news...he's on his way to becoming a big wheel!"

Eggs-Acting Economics

BY WILLMA WILLIS GORE OF PORTERVILLE, CALIFORNIA

I didn't know what I was starting when I asked Charlie to pick up a flat of eggs at the feed store. First, he raved about the cost. ("I can remember when you got a dozen free with a slab of bacon!") Then he made one of those grand, time-to-economize decisions that come every year between fall harvest and spring planting.

We were going to buy some chickens so we'd have our own eggs and fryers. That "we" translated into "Charlie-language" means, "I'll start it; you get to take care of it."

Actually, it's my early-in-life acquaintance with chickens that has kept me from suggesting we raise them here. My folks had a flock on the little dairy where I grew up. They ran free, scrounging most of their own food, and the hens always laid away.

My mother was a virtual ferret when it came to finding their nests, and she was a study in foxy efficiency when she wanted a fryer or stewing hen for Sunday dinner—the bird was ready for plucking by the time the teakettle came to a boil.

But I have absolutely no aspirations to add chicken raising to my calf-feeding and Charlie-tending jobs at this late date. I wouldn't mind a few laying hens, penned, but no free-lance flocks and no meat birds! There's nothing quite so economical as poultry under plastic, ready for the oven.

However, Charlie—once the bit's between his teeth—is hard to rein in. It took him only a few hours to fence a small space and clear the old chicken house of its 20-year accumulation of baling wire.

In a couple of days, the classifieds rewarded him with an ad: "Fourteen laying hens; one rooster. For Sale." He arranged to pick them up that night. I silently scheduled rooster stew as the initial benefit from Charlie's purchase but agreed to go along to help bag the birds.

We set out right after dinner, taking my little car because of its economical gas mileage. Charlie paid for the chickens, assuring the owner that we could manage the capture if he'd just point out the hen house. I carried binding twine and five grain sacks we'd brought along and followed Charlie and his flashlight lead.

At the hen house door, he gave me the torch. I was to direct the beam into the eye of each bird, causing temporary blindness so he could grab it.

The theory is good, but when the first hen—blinded or not—feels hands on her wings, and if the hands don't simultaneously grab

51

her throat, her protesting squawk starts an escalating bedlam among the lot.

"The eye, the eye!" Charlie hissed as I tried to zero in with the light on the next chicken and at the same time protect my face from the flock, whose frantic attempts to escape were no better coordinated than my aim with the flashlight. Besides making beam-to-eye contact, I was also supposed to hold the sack open, count three birds per sack, and with my third and fourth hands keep the twine untangled and tie the openings!

Charlie had blocked the hen house exit with a board, so eventually we captured all 15. I knew I'd "mis-bagged" them when the last sack held only one bird, but it seemed immaterial at that moment.

Charlie carried three sacks; I, the other two and the flashlight. I hurried ahead, wanting to get the smelly birds into and out of my car trunk as fast as possible. We sped back home and by the light of the flashlight, emptied our dazed flock into the darkness of their new house.

The next morning Charlie drove out early to pick up a coupling for the stock trailer. Once again, he took my car for economy's sake. I, of course, was assigned to feed our new charges.

"The poor rooster, my foot—the last time I saw him he was crossing Main Street against the light!"

Out at the pen, I filled the tray with grain and was pleased to see them peck eagerly, but I wondered instantly what kind of a rancher would think that any of these was a rooster. There were four Barred Rocks, four Plymouth Rocks and six Rhode Island Reds—all pullets. Then I realized that these numbers didn't total 15.

I checked inside the hen house. Nothing. Obviously, the rooster was missing.

Suddenly I remembered that one bird had soloed in the sack race last night and must still be in the trunk of the car, certainly suffocated by now and—regardless of my personal feelings—undeserving of such a fate.

Back at the house, I listened for Charlie's return and ran out to meet him as he pulled into the driveway. The moment he stopped, I was at the car window. "Charlie, we must have left one of the birds in the trunk last night. What a horrible death!"

"Death, my foot!" he fumed. "That rooster nearly gave me

a heart attack. The last I saw of him, he was crossing Main Street against the light.''

I was relieved. The rooster's chances with the traffic were better than with me as keeper of the stew pot. So long as Charlie doesn't get it into his head to find a replacement rooster, I can put up with the hens.

And I won't bother to explain to him that with feed and shell, minerals, louse and mite medications, time off for moulting and going ''broody''...our hens' eggs probably won't cost more than a couple of dollars a dozen!

Oh, For a Few Minutes Alone!

By Jo Edgington of Lebanon, Tennessee

I f there's one thing farm life supplies a lot of, it's *togetherness.* Dad, the kids, the neighbors…at least one of them always seems to be around. And if by some miracle they've gone their separate ways and I grab a second cup of coffee, the phone rings. What's a farm woman to do?

Don't get me wrong, I enjoy being with my family. But there are times when I enjoy being with myself, too. Yet invariably I become Bo Peep with the rest of the family following behind.

My togetherness quandry came to a boiling point one night as I cooked supper. Thinking I was all alone, I raced from the stove to the refrigerator—only to trip over my son's No. 9 feet. I spun around in the other direction…only to collide with daughter Sheri Lyn. Suddenly I realized that the entire family had gathered around the kitchen table, their legs stretched half way across the room, as they munched my first batch of fried okra like popcorn.

It was then I knew I needed a solution that would yield solitude. Politely put them to work, I reasoned. That should chase them out fast. Sure enough, after a few assignments they avoided the kitchen like poison ivy. Now they sneak the fried okra as they dash through and dart out the back door before I can shout "Set the table".

Unfortunately not all togetherness happens at mealtime. Did you ever have one of those days when everybody talks constantly, yet says nothing? Or asks endless questions like "What are you doing?" and "Why?". Or better still, "I don't understand the movie on TV. Mom, will you explain it to me" (How could I *possibly* explain it when I'm in another room washing the windows?)

It was one of *those* days that I almost blurted out "get lost" when *I* decided to "get lost" instead. What a perfect time to hoe the garden, I thought—and though weeds make me itch, at least they can't talk. I knew the kids wouldn't follow me *there,* but just to make sure, I took an extra hoe and propped it against the fence. At last I'd found the ideal scarecrow for would be chatterers. (For some strange reason that summer we had the cleanest garden in the neighborhood.)

But, alas, the first killing frost wilted my hideaway and a new solution was necessary. One rainy Saturday in late fall I knew something had to be done—*fast.* My daughter turned cartwheels for 2 hours across the living room floor, and my son clanked barbells while his stereo rattled the roof. Those kids couldn't have heard even if I'd *tried* to yell "Get quiet!"

So I decided to fight noise *with* noise. Usually I put off my Saturday head-washing since my thick hair requires a minimum "frying" time of an hour under the dryer. But this being an emergency, I welcomed the occasion...for nothing, absolutely nothing, could outroar that antique hair dryer. Finally, clenching *Farm Woman* in my left hand and a cup of coffee in my right, I enjoyed such peace and quiet!

There comes a time, however, when my hair doesn't need washing, no loud vacuuming has to be done, the plants have died in the garden, supper is finished and the solutions become more exhausting than they're worth. Not to be defeated, I play one last trump! I give in to togetherness, turn around and with a great big hug (maybe even a kiss) I admit how much I enjoy my family's company after all.

At such times my preteen daughter hugs me right back, makes me feel loved all over, then runs off. The teenager? He scrams in a hurry. My husband goes into stunned silence from the shock and staggers off. And somehow during that short, miraculous solitude, I wonder why I bothered with the other solutions in the first place!

New Barber in Town

BY GWEN TARBELL OF NORTH FRYEBURG, MAINE

My great-grandmother always said there was Indian blood in the family, and my long-standing barbering desire proved her right. For years I had suggested to my husband, Roger, that he let me cut his hair.

I used all the arguments I could think of: "You could avoid all those special trips into town," I'd tell him. "There would be no long wait...think of the money you'd save."

Nothing worked. Then the price of haircuts rose, and Roger finally consented to let me at him.

Before he changed his mind, I dashed out and bought a home barber set. I read the directions carefully, then coaxed Roger into

---

"The clippers hummed in my hand, and hair started to fall like snow. Suddenly they slipped... and Roger squirmed uneasily!"

---

the chair. (He was about to bolt until I reassured him that my mother was dropping in later, and if anything should go wrong—but of course it wouldn't—she could *probably* fix it.)

Finally calmed, Roger allowed me to place the apron around his neck. I clutched the clippers and turned them on.

They hummed softly in my hand, and hair started to fall like snow. Roger squirmed in the chair. Hoping to calm his nerves, I began to sing. Right in the middle of my excellent imitation of Perry Como, the clippers slipped—just a little.

Roger attempted a 180° turn in the chair and blurted out, "When a barber cuts hair, he does..."

I interrupted him to point out that I wasn't a barber, and that wasn't what the directions said to do.

"Are you sure your mother's coming over today?" his voice quivered.

I switched to the shears and snipped away happily.

"When a barber cuts hair..." Roger began again. At that point I contemplated a general anesthetic but decided it'd be unethical.

To dampen Roger's spirits even more, our hound, "Snoopy", ambled into the kitchen, took one look at Roger, ducked his head and crept out.

"What's the matter with the dog?" Roger queried.

"Oh, he always looks mournful, you know that!"

But Roger wasn't convinced, and he made another inquiry about my mother. By now his fidgeting had grown worse, and he bobbed around like a yo-yo as I tried to snip away "loose ends".

"If you don't sit still, there won't be anything for Mom to fix," I gruffly noted, picking up the clippers again for the final touch— the results of which scared even me a little.

I combed and combed while Roger chomped at the bit to take a look.

"It's done!" I announced finally.

Roger bounded from his chair and sprinted for the bathroom. Soon I heard sobs and a stream of mumbling.

Shortly Roger stormed back into the kitchen, slapped on his hat—which immediately sank to his ears—and blurted out, "I'm going to the barn. Call me when your mother gets here!"

I watched his long neck and big ears disappear. Then, with a sigh, I shoveled up the hair, wondering why my dear husband didn't at least leave a tip!

Old MacDonald Sheds His Disguise

BY JANIS HARRISON OF WINDSOR, MISSOURI

When I accepted my husband's proposal of marriage, I had no idea that lurking beneath the surface of his kind and thoughtful exterior was "Old MacDonald".

Sure, I knew my caring husband had a fondness for animals. Before we were married, he had an aquarium and a small flock of chickens. Was this enough to make me suspicious? Of course not. I had grown up on a farm, and we had chickens, too, plus the usual dog and cats.

That his small flock could blossom into a menagerie didn't occur to me. To this day, I think it was the purchase of 10 acres outside of town that brought his lurking passion to the surface. All of a sudden I was married to Old MacDonald...with a "cluck cluck here" and a "gobble gobble there" we were surrounded.

Not only did we acquire cats, a dog, more chickens, ducks, geese, turkeys and guineas, but also three goat kids. I was assured they were quite harmless, and reluctantly I agreed they were cute with their soft brown eyes and loppy ears. But like all cuddly pets, these too grew into large adults.

Goats possess a dual personality, I learned. One minute they can be frolicking over the roof of your new car and the next grazing passively on the fresh green grass. They can clear an acre of elm sprouts or nibble the delectable tips of poison ivy, all without any sign of indigestion.

It was their huge appetite that held me in awe...and led to our forced (by me) separation.

A good stout fence surrounding our property was on our list of priorities when we moved to the farm, but so far it hadn't appeared. The chickens had their home and a run. The other animals stayed near the pond. As for the goats, we had four steel panels tied together forming a large pen that we moved each day to give them plenty of fresh grazing.

One afternoon when we came home from town, we found our goats had literally scaled the walls of their home and escaped into the unsuspecting world. I was content to write them off as "good riddance" but not my husband. We searched our 10 acres for hours calling those goats.

"Here, Buttons!" "Here, Billy!" "Here, Nanny!" But no bleat returned our call.

Thoroughly disgusted, we went back to the house to find the telephone ringing. My husband answered, and I could tell by the red blush creeping up his neck it wasn't a social call.

"All afternoon," he muttered.

"Oh, Oh," he repeated several times.

I knew our social standing in the neighborhood had hit rock bottom when he said, "And they ate it to the ground!"

I closed my eyes wearily. Knowing those goats as well as I did I knew their meal could consist of anything from a clothesline pole to a 40-ft. oak tree.

My husband hung up the phone and slowly turned to me. With eyes lowered, he explained.

Apparently our footloose friends decided plain old grass was too tame for their gourmet diet. They had hopped across the boundary line on the north and proceeded to wander 4 miles to the garden of a little, old widow lady. It wasn't just any garden but her rose garden, full of roses to be entered that very weekend in the county fair. She always won first place—this year, thanks to our goats, would be the first time in 12 years she wouldn't have an entry.

She had gone on to say that our goats hadn't just eaten the perfect blooms but had continued down the thorny stems until they were rubbing their noses into the straw mulch around the hybrids' roots. She had slipped a noose around their necks, and at present they were fertilizing her front porch. Would we like to come get them?

I was all for changing our name and moving into the next county, but hubby thought that would be the coward's way out.

So suddenly I had entirely too much to do around the house. He went alone to make our apologies and to retrieve the culprits.

As for our neighbor we continued to have a nodding acquaintance with her, but things never progressed beyond that point. She wouldn't accept payment for the damage. In fact, she seemed to shudder if we brought up the subject of restitution. We let the matter drop. The goats were placed in a more secure pen, and we tried to forget the unforgettable.

As I write this, the goats are gone as is "10 acres". We have a larger place and more animals. Our menagerie has grown to include sheep, cows and hogs, along with the assorted poultry.

We still have to occasionally return escapees to their pens, but none like those goats. Theirs was a truly memorable run for the roses!

The Saga of Molly Hatchet...
(OR Why I Vetoed Cattle Ranching)

By Iona Maricelli of Daingerfield, Texas

Mom! I've found me a calf!" Mike's eyes were wide with excitement as my 15-year-old ran into the kitchen. "I talked to Floyd Michaels, and he just bought some calves at an auction and he said I could buy one from him. He even said I could have my pick. Boy, I'm gonna pick out the biggest one there!"

My heart sank! You see, I had already been through first year FFA and had a good idea of what I was in for. Things like "Mom, the school bus is early—would you put out feed and water just today?"...or "But I couldn't find the curry comb; I didn't think you'd mind if I used your hairbrush."

But Mike *had* to have a project, so it was arranged for him and his dad to drive over to the Michaels place and pick out his calf on Saturday morning.

All week the only thing Mike could talk about was that calf. "Boy, I can't wait! This year I know I'm going to get a ribbon!"

When Saturday finally rolled around, nobody had to wake the

"Something made that calf stand out from the crowd...maybe it was how he snorted, pawed the ground and glared with half-crazed eyes!"

---

boy. As a matter of fact, he almost wore a path in the kitchen floor from the table to the back door waiting for his dad to finish his coffee. Finally they were off, and I looked forward to a peaceful morning—something the men, I learned later, wouldn't have.

Floyd met them in the front yard, and the three walked over to take a look at the 30 calves milling around in the Texas dust. My cautious husband thought to himself as they approached the pen, "There's no way the boy is going to pick out a good one from this lot of scrubs."

But Mike jumped on the fence and crawled to the top rail. "That's him, that's the one I was telling you about," he shouted.

There was something about the calf that made him stand out. It wasn't his size, though he was a little larger than the others...nor his scruffy, nondescript brindle coat...or his knock-kneed appear-

61

ance. Maybe it *was* the way he lowered his head, snorted, pawed the ground and glared with half-crazed eyes!

"Are you sure that's the one you want? There's a pretty good looking Hereford over there," Dad tried. But nothing would do. Mike had to have the brindle.

Getting him was another matter, however. After about the fourth attempt at placing a rope on the calf, the men finally gave up and herded the critter into the chute, where he immediately lay down and wedged himself under the bottom rail on the fence. All attempts to unwedge him were useless until Floyd took a cutting torch to the steel rail.

At last, after much sweat—and near tears from Mike—the calf was loaded and on his way home. (This behavior should have told the guys something—but no!)

The unloading was nearly as bad as the loading. If it had not been for the heavy rope tied securely around the calf's nose, there

---

"The joke around the ranch was the calf would fight a circle saw given the chance!"

---

would have been a first-class rodeo in our yard. As it was, it took two grown men and a teenage boy to maneuver the calf out of the trailer and tie him to a fence rail.

"You'll need to leave that calf tied up there for 2 or 3 days till he gentles down a bit," Floyd cautioned as he walked over to his pickup. "Good luck. We'll be seein' ya," he grinned as he drove away.

Eight days later there was still no hope of even touching that wild-eyed critter. It was all anyone could do to get close enough to shove a bucket of feed and some water in front of him.

The only one in the family undaunted by all this was Mike. He was still determined that he would have a top show calf. His dad and I just shook our heads.

About this time, Mike named the beast "Molly Hatchet". No one knew why, though the standard joke around our ranch was that he would fight a circle saw given the chance. But the name seemed to fit, so it stuck.

Just feeding and watering Molly was an adventure, but little by little the calf did gentle enough that Mike could put hands on him. Finally, after a month, Molly was fighting the lead halter.

One memorable day Dad decided that maybe Molly would

62

earn to lead safer and easier if he were tied to the bumper of the old pickup. During the first try, Molly sat down and attempted to stop the pickup, plowing the ground all the way. When the truck stopped of its own accord, Molly jerked the rope in two and dared anyone to come near him. He stood with head lowered, pawing little billows of dust. That was when Mike and Dad both decided that steer wrestling wasn't their sport.

After months of our sweating and straining over Molly Hatchet, show time arrived. What we didn't realize was our calf's escapades had just begun.

Molly had never been around a crowd, and because of his contrary disposition we decided a call to the vet for tranquilizers was

---

"The calf tried to climb the nearest light pole and tangled himself in a guy wire!"

---

in order. He gave them to Mike to feed Molly in the morning, and we were lulled into thinking things would go well.

And they did...until the men actually drove in at the show grounds. Immediately Molly's eyes rolled and saliva poured from his mouth as he flung his head back and forth and bawled at the top of his lungs.

Two men who had been standing nearby ran over to see if they could help unload the calf. That was their first mistake! Wild-eyed, Molly came unglued the minute his feet hit the ground. He tried to climb back into the trailer using the sideboards as a ladder. When that failed, he jerked loose from the three men who were holding him and fled toward the grandstands.

That animal *had* to be a show calf—everyone in the stands saw him...and ran for dear life!

Finally several people herded Molly back toward the trailer. But they didn't quite make it before he decided to climb a light pole and tangle himself in a guy wire.

Miracles do happen, however. The tranquilizers finally took effect, and the men put another rope on Molly. Then five strong men tugged him to the trailer, where another tranquilizer awaited.

I really don't think it's necessary to say that neither Mike nor Molly received even honorable mention—but I'll bet Molly was definitely "mentioned" in many conversations the next few weeks!

After that, I vowed my son could raise anything from a shark to a boa constrictor for his FFA project—just no more cattle!

MORE GOOD RURAL READING!

OUR first edition of *Why Farm Wives Age Fast* was such a success
it led to the second edition you're now holding in your hands. After
chuckling through that first book, readers implored us to add this
second volume to their library.

If you're one of the few fans of this second edition who hasn't as
yet seen that first edition, we're telling you right here that you can
order a copy...and it's just as funny as this one.

If you like this second edition, you'll *love* the first edition of this
book series that has people laughing out loud across rural America.
0211 *Why Farm Wives Age Fast* book (No. 1) **$4.95**

**THE MOST EMBARRASSING MOMENTS OF FARMERS AND
RANCHERS.** Ever say or do something so *embarrassing* that years
later you *still* blush about it? If you've ever felt that small, you'll close-
ly identify with—and find laughs galore in—*The Most Embarrassing
Moments of Farmers and Ranchers*.

This popular new book brings together some of the *funniest* red-
faced rural recollections you'll find anywhere...and they're all told
directly by the folks who did the blushing first!

It's a book you'll read over and over again!
0368 *Most Embarrassing Moments* **$4.95**

THE GRANDMA & GRANDPA BOOKS, I & II. Each book in this
collection overflows with nostalgic stories about farm and ranch life.

Warm stories and touching photos take readers back to the time
of cooking for threshers, hitching up the team and Sunday "go to
meetin' " clothes. Folks with fond farm backgrounds will find themselves smiling broadly one moment, shedding a tear the next as they
"listen" to the reminiscences of dozens of farm and ranch "Grand-
mas and Grandpas". Each big book is value-priced at only $5.95
(which makes it a great gift from grandkids) or you can order all four
for the super-saver price of just $19.95! Use codes as listed below.

0221 *Grandma Book I* **$5.95**	**0220** *Grandpa Book I* **$5.95**
0257 *Grandma Book II* **$5.95**	**0258** *Grandpa Book II* **$5.95**
0241 Deluxe Combo, one each of all four books *(you save $3.85!)* . . **$19.95**

TO ORDER these books or additional copies of *Why Farm Wives Age Fast,
No. II* (Code 0367, $4.95), write your name and address on a slip of paper
along with the code number, title, quantity and price of each book ordered.
(Please add $1 postage/handling for each book ordered.) Mail with payment
to: Country Store, Suite 1351, 5925 Country Lane, Greendale WI 53129.